Nature Do

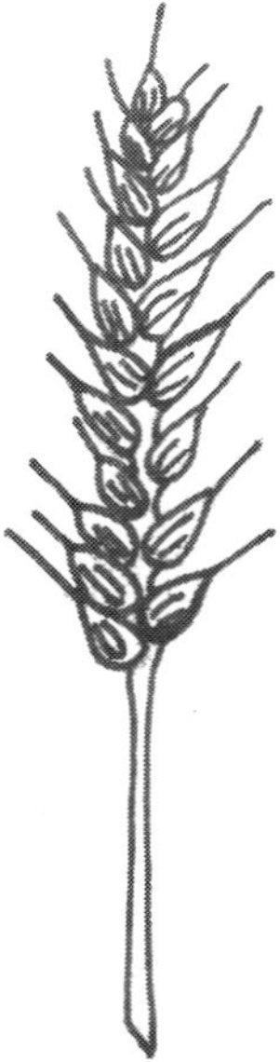

Front cover drawing: Pine resin was traditionally mixed with soot and walnut oil to produce printing inks. I once visited a monastery in the foothills of the Himalayas whose monks collected it for their small printing press.

Copyright © Uttrang Kaur Khalsa 2017

Published by Pomegranate Press
South Chailey, Lewes, Sussex BN8 4QB
www.pomegranate-press.co.uk

ISBN: 978-1-907242-63-2

Printed by 4Edge, Eldon Way, Hockley, Essex SS5 4AD

WHY ENJOY THIS BOOK ?

The natural choice means prosperity for all pockets.

*We all like to do green and ethical good deeds
for our countryside when we can.*

"Jevehe karma kamaavadaa tevehe phalate"

ONE OBTAINS FRUITS ACCORDING TO THE DEEDS
WHICH HE DOES.

Siri Guru Granth, Ang 317

Natural Bathroom Beauty

❋❋❋❋❋❋❋❋❋❋❋❋❋❋❋

Natural deodorants

(WHAT OUR GREAT-GRANDMOTHERS USED TO USE)

Potato – helpfully absorbs heat and smells. Cut a potato in half and rub it under your arm.

Radish – cut and rub as above

Turnip – *ditto*

Bay leaf – drying and lovely smelling.

Lemon – my friend loves this in hot weather!

Lovage – boil the leaves or root in a pan.
Simmer for five minutes. Cool and store in a clean jar.
To use, soak a cotton cloth or cotton wool
in the deodorising liquid.

LIP CARE

Kind enough to eat – Yummy!

*Snuggling in with what the goddess of the earth offers us
to be beautiful, we commit a good karma eco-deed.
All health, wealth, happiness and beauty
is a result of our karma.*

Orange peel: the white inside of an orange or tangerine peel contains rutin which works as a wonderful moisturiser and exfoliator all in one. Simply save your orange peel and wipe the inside of it across your lips.

Olive oil: use the best organic quality olive oil as a lip moisturiser.

Mashed strawberries: a delight in summer for natural strawberry colour! Stored in a little pot, they can last for many days – and longer if you mix them with olive oil or ghee.

Beetroot powder: add beetroot powder to shea butter or cocoa butter or ghee. For a browner colour add cocoa.

FACIAL CLEANSERS

Cucumber
Water melon
Pineapple
Banana
Strawberry
Papaya
Apple
Cold camomile tea

Breath freshener

It's easy to carry fennel seeds or a green chili in your handbag to chew on.

Some people put fresh sage, parsley or basil in a little box as an alternative to chemical chewing gum or breath mints full of E numbers.

Natural Aromatherapy Everywhere

Aromatherapy is the art of being healed by smell

Body knowledge: The mūlādhāra chakra (the root chakra) is affiliated to the sense of smell.

Music Knowledge: Sa in Indian music (approximately our note C) also relates to the mūlādhāra chakra.

The jnana-indriya or organ of knowledge is the nose, according to ancient Indian texts.

Smelling and listening can open and clear the root chakra, which is the 'basis of fears' chakra. In every moment an aware being is aware of the sense of smell.

Tooth powder
(DIY toothpaste pick and mix)

Comfrey root
(also usable as a toothbrush, as liquorice root is)
Black pepper
Rose petal powder
Oak leaf
Mint powder
Charcoal
Bilberry powder
Thyme powder
Rosemary powder

How to use a tooth powder

Store your powder in a little box.

Open and sprinkle a tooth fairy amount of powder into the palm of your hand.

Run your tooth brush under water so it is wet with happiness.

Dab the wet toothbrush into the tooth powder and massage gently.

If the cupboard looks sparse the simplest DIY toothpaste could be salt . . . In the Himalayas a yogic taught me to employ just earth – Mother Nature's vault

NATURAL TOOTH BRUSHES

The twigs of trees are used by Nihang Sikhs, some wandering yogis, wild-living bushmen and a few European gypsies

United Kingdom, Europe & United States
Apple
Pear
Fig
Hazelnut
Orange
Lime
Silver birch

Australia
Mango Tree, Magousteen Tree, Orange Tree

India
Pilu (*Salvadora Persica*)
Neem
Kicker
Peepal tree
The Indian plum or ber fruit tree
The Java plum or jamun tree
Gum arabic tree
Bael tree
Dhak
Madar ak
Mango

Trees tend to your tendrils

(Plastic *vs* wooden combs)

Chinese and Japanese doctors recommend wood combs as a cure for restoring health, good memory and peace of mind.
All Sikhs comb their hair with wooden combs.
Some administer different kinds of woods as remedies, combing their hair as a meditation in the morning and evening.

Trees are a symbol of the Earth's supreme wisdom.

Peach wood is very feminine, abundant and light – like a peach laughing in summertime.

Cherry wood is good for the heart; for peace of mind.

Olive wood is a symbol of the holy spirit – thought to aid meditation

Sandalwood is healing, cooling, peaceful and so generously saintly she cools the fevers in snakes who love to rest in her branches.

Combing is good for the nervous system (hair is said to be an extension of it) and it stimulates the brain's neuron replacement.

Natural Soaps and Shampoos

A good question to ask of a hair
or body cleanser: Would you eat it?

SOAPWORT. THE SOAPY SOLUTION CAN ALSO BE USED TO WASH CLOTHES. SOME PEOPLE USE THE WHOLE PLANT AND SOME JUST THE ROOT. SOME PEOPLE ADD LEMON VERBENA OR ROSE PETALS, LAVENDER OR CAMOMILE FOR LOVELY SMELLING LAUNDRY.

HOME MADE **YOGURT** FULL OF HELPFUL BACTERIA: POUR ON, LEAVE ON FOR 10 MINUTES, THEN RINSE.

WHEY MILK AND GHEE. THIS IS AN ANCIENT FORMULA FROM SACRED SIKH SPIRITUAL TEXTS WHICH SAY IT IS PERMISSIBLE TO WASH YOUR HAIR WITH WHEY MILK AND GHEE AND DRY IT IN THE SUNSHINE EVERY TWO WEEKS — AND ALSO TO CELEBRATE YOUR HAIR LIKE THE GURU BY PUTTING FLOWERS IN IT.

CHARCOAL, PURE CLAY OR MUD. YOU COULD ALSO CLEAN HAIR WITH FIREWOOD ASH. SOME PEOPLE ADD HERBS TO THEIR MIXTURE.

NETTLE. A FEW CRUSHED NETTLES LIKE A NETTLE TEA.

RYE. BOIL A FEW TABLESPOONS OF RYE FLOUR IN WATER. WHEN COOLED , MIX WELL - THIS LIQUID PASTE IS CLEANSING

Natural Supplements and Vitamins

THERE IS A NATURAL VERSION OF EVERYTHING
MANY PEOPLE REPORT THAT THE FRESH VERSION IS HEALTH BOOSTING

Vitamin C = oranges, broccoli, tomatoes, kiwi fruit, strawberries, blackberries and many more

Vitamin A = carrots, sweet potatoes, dark leafy greens, grapefruit, mango, melon, water melon

Zen Travel Light Towel Philosophy

How many towels have you got?

Could they be handwoven cotton which doubles up as a shawl for lightweight travel?

Can you do your towel washing by hand?

Make up - kind enough to eat

EYE MAKE-UP – Did you know that you can use coca powder as brown eyeshadow and oil lamp soot as kohl, just like a goddess yogini from the Himalayas?

Natural soot kohl is part of a daily ritual that protects the eyes of yoginis.

If you can eat your beauty products they are generally kinder. Play around with natural colour powders such as hibiscus or coca and see what you can swap in your make-up bag to be kinder to the Earth.

Natural Skin Scrubbing!

Dry brushing with natural plant bristles such as cactus bristles which are made into body brushes or with hay made into a wisp.

How to make a hay wisp for body brushing: dampen long strands of hay and twist together to make a long rope. When the rope is long enough (about 6ft or so) make two loops at one end; pass the rest of the rope around one loop and then the other to weave it together; tuck the end well in – job done!

Nature lovers make sugar scrubs with the most natural sugar you can find. Explore cotton bags filled with oats . . . in circular motions.

HERBAL BATH WATER SOAKS

Lavender, Camomile . . . What can you grow to soak with?

(Saving one plastic bottle is a act of Earth goodness)

Natural moisturiser

Mashed avocado?
Home-grown aloe vera?
Olive oil?

(Simple solutions for hundreds of years)

FOOT WASHING

An old Indian proverb says that those who wash their feet before bed are devoted, healthy and wise.

Here are some extras to add to your foot wash

FOR COLD FEET:
GINGER
ROSE HIPS
CLOVES
BAY LEAVES
ORANGE PEEL
JUNIPER BERRIES/DAMSON BERRIES/CRANBERRIES

FOR HOT FEET:
MINT
CUCUMBER
GRAPEFRUIT
CAMOMILE
LIME FLOWER BLOSSOM
BASIL

Help Your feet breathe

Yogis and reflexologists teach us that we can be healed
through the feet.

So, try to take your shoes and socks off while sitting
at your work or at home, and see if the reports of better posture,
circulation, sensitivity through stimulation works for you, too.

Connect to the earth – put your feet on a natural material
(for example, an organic cotton rug, cork mat or grass mat).

100 per cent cotton socks are biodegradable and more breathable.

Natural Mouth Wash

Rosemary mouth wash:

Fresh rosemary sprigs
A couple of cloves (optional)
Pure water

Place cloves and rosemary in water and simmer until infused.
Allow to cool, and strain.

Natural Hair Care

Sikhs, Yogis (such as Milarepa)
and Native American Indians
never cut their hair . . .

There is no need to cut!

Natural Fashion

For your consideration... Many of us wear cloths such as flax or cotton coloured naturally

BROWN: dandelion roots, oak bark, walnut hulls, tea, coffee, acorns.

PINK: berries, cherries, red and pink roses, avocado skins and seeds (*really!*)

RED-BROWN: pomegranates, beets, bamboo, hibiscus (reddish colour flowers), bloodroot

ORANGE: carrots, gold lichen, onion skins

YELLOW: bay leaves, marigolds, sunflower petals, St John's wort, dandelion flowers, turmeric.

GREEN: artichokes, spinach, peppermint leaves, snapdragons, lilacs, grass, nettles, peach leaves.

BLUE: indigo, woad, red cabbage, elderberries, red mulberries, blueberries, purple grapes.

RED-PURPLE: red sumac berries, basil leaves, day lilies, pokeweed berries, huckleberries

Choosing natural cloths is a sign that you care for the earth.

Menstrual Mindfulness

Washable reusable cotton or flax pads — there are many eco brands.

Or sew your own . . .

Our parts breathe!

Which is more natural for a baby's sensitive bottom –
cotton hand-tied nappies
or a large pack of plastic?

simple sewing

100 per cent cotton thread *vs* polyester

Wooden buttons *vs* plastic

Hand-sewing *vs* electronic machine

Shoes

Espadrille grass soles? Natural tree rubber? Cotton?

A question for vegetarians: Is leather or sheepskin kinder and more in harmony with nature than plastic pollution?

(Whimsy: Could a baby bunny call it home?)

Bag

Wooden buttons *vs* drawstrings *vs* machine-made zips?

Can you grow and compost the fabric in a garden?

What's the eco talking point?

Hand-sewing meditation

A functional mala or rosary?

What are you doing with your time – and why does it prevent you from sewing one outfit a year?

HAND-KNITTED?

Kindly combed wool:
with a natural knitting needle
and by the grace of wool from a cashmere goat
we can all be self-sustainably warm . . .

(Goat breeds can be hand-combed for wool
instead of sheared.)

Home-grown cloth

I have a friend who grows flax in her garden which she then spins and knits into clothes!

NATURAL LAUNDRY SOAP

Soapwort can be grown in the garden next to the kitchen herbs

Whimsy of the page:

Could an insect safely swim through your cleaning solution?

an ethical consideration

**Plant half an acre of trees
to offset one year of car driving.**

(Source: Science 2.0 – mathematical statistics for the environment)

ੴ

Ik Ong Kar

One Creator Does

Sikhs believe that there is One God or Mr Universe or One United Creator Deity (so Buddha and Jesus are equally pervaded by ONE God)